# good bones, great pieces

The seven essential pieces that will carry you through a lifetime

# good bones, great pieces

Suzanne & Lauren McGrath

PHOTOGRAPHS BY LUCAS ALLEN

STEWART, TABORI & CHANG
NEW YORK

# DEDICATION

To Kaye, mother, grandmother, and proud homekeeper, who taught us that it's okay to move things around in life as long as the core pieces are meaningful and bring you happiness.

# ACKNOWLEDGMENTS

There were many people who helped us write this book. Our deepest thanks to: LUCAS ALLEN, for capturing our concept with so much thoughtfulness and precision; ALICE TAIT, illustrator extraordinaire, for being such an integral part of the creative process; ANDREA BARVZI, our agent at ICM, for believing in our idea and fighting for us from day one; DERVLA KELLY, our editor at Abrams, for giving us the incredible opportunity; NATASHA LOUISE KING for her unquestionable eye—even from long distance; AMY SLY for her ability to lay out the pages so artfully; JODY KIVORT for his humor and calm under fire; MEREDITH GERMAN and ROSS WENDELL for sharing their adorable apartment with us; JANICE and MARSHALL KNOPF for the opportunity to design in their exceptional spaces; DIANA HEALD for turning over her first apartment to us; DR. STEPHEN and KRISTEN FEALY for inviting us to photograph their beloved apartment just days before moving out; MICHAEL and LISA HUGHES for letting us in and answering all of our questions about their amazing Chinese antiquities; EVE KRYZANOWSKI for her pivotal introductions and ingenuity; KEVIN SHARKEY for his readiness to lend a hand; HELOISE GOODMAN for skillfully recommending Lucas; our friends at ABC Carpet & Home, ALIZA OLIN and JESSICA CATALANO, for their willingness to work with us and for their enthusiasm for the project; SHEILA CUTNER for providing a wise second opinion on everything; JODI KAHN for her friendship and expertise; MOLLY PETERS for her spirited support; PAUL LUTHRINGER for his media know-how; KATHARINA PLATH for her boundless enthusiasm; ZAN GOODMAN for her sharp eye and inspired creative direction; BRADLEY HUGHES for his exceptional advice; JULIANA RIBEIRO for being a sounding board and a great friend; LOTTE MEISTER for her accessorizing adroitness; MADELINE COLL for her skillful assistance; MARTHA STEWART for her inspiration and friendship; and AMY ASTLEY for her mentorship and kindness.

To the designers who contributed their knowledge and expertise: ROBERT COUTURIER for his genius and generosity; MILES REDD for demonstrating how to be fearless with color; LIEN LUU for her effortless melding of unexpected objects; BARRIE BENSON for her ease in creating an updated take on Dorothy Draper; and GARROW KEDIGIAN for his intelligence, elegance, and candor.

To the members of our immediate family: MATT McGRATH for traveling with us to Brimfield, Massachusetts, to capture the joy we take in finding great pieces; PATRICK REILLY for being our in-house editor and head of the tea-and-tech department; and JACK REILLY for supplying endless affection to his mom and big sister throughout.

# CONTENTS

*Suzanne*   I had once again brought my daughter to a job site. I was in my thirties, newly single, standing in the parlor of a brownstone in Brooklyn Heights. I had my own business as an interior designer, and my client needed a decision. I was trying to choose which of three variations of a yellow paint would work. Square samples were painted on the wall and labeled one, two, and three. I hesitated. And then, from behind me, a tiny voice announced with confidence, "Number two. It's the palest and shines like the sun." From that day on, I knew that Lauren and I would collaborate and that she would be the one choosing the paint colors.

*LAUREN*   I went to college in Maine, and down the road was an old factory that had been turned into an antiques warehouse. My mom came to visit me more than any of my classmates' parents did. Why? Because Maine has great antiquing. We walked each aisle of that warehouse, sifting through decades of collectibles. There were the kitschy red lobster-claw salt and pepper shakers she bought me after my first breakup, the painting of sheep she gave me when I suffered from a bout of insomnia, and the woven blanket she found that my friends and I picnicked on all senior year out on the quad. From my childhood home to my dorm room to my first apartment, these pieces gave me comfort and reflected our combined sense of style. My friends couldn't figure out how my mom did it. But they all wanted her to show them how.

# INTRODUCTION

With all the changing, moving, and reinventing going on these days, it's never been more important to make a home and to choose the right furniture pieces for it that can stay with you through it all. We're talking about indispensable pieces that you love today and you'll still love fifteen years from now. Making a home truly is a lifelong pursuit.

The question of what furniture to buy and where it should go in the home is something everyone struggles with. The obvious pieces, like the bed, the kitchen table, and the sofa are easy enough. But what about the pieces that give your home personality and flair, and, once you find them, where do they fit in best?

That's where we come in. In a world where there is a dizzying array of choices, we've narrowed it all down to seven essential pieces that are so timeless, chic, and flexible that you'll always find a place (or two or three or four!) for them. Our goal is to help you create rooms that always look fresh and inspired by using an inventory of key pieces that have the ability to move from room to room and home to home.

We aren't the first to think the whole process is overwhelming. In her highly amusing 1939 book, *Decorating Is Fun!*—gotta love that title—Dorothy Draper quotes Mrs. Theodore Roosevelt, Jr.: "Every woman in her secret heart believes herself to be a potential interior decorator, but usually when she gets started, she loses her nerve. . . . She becomes confused by the great variety of material that confronts her when she shops. She loses confidence, becomes timid, and falls back on the drab and mediocre because she is afraid of doing wrong."

The idea for this book grew out of our blog, goodbonesgreatpieces.com. We were inspired by the thousands of comments and e-mails from our readers asking for home-decorating advice. Our book is written for women of all

ages—from single women moving into their first apartments to young women establishing themselves in their grown-up "thirty-something" spaces to new moms balancing families and careers and even to empty nesters who are looking for inspiration and sound, budget-friendly advice.

In the pages of this book you'll find spaces decorated by us, but also by many interior designers who share our point of view. Rooms designed by celebrated decorators Miles Redd, Robert Couturier, Garrow Kedigian, Lien Luu, and Barrie Benson showcase each of the seven pieces in thoughtful and often

unconventional ways. They offer insights to the how and why of choosing great pieces, as well as many helpful tips gathered from years of experience.

For us, decorating is not about the quick fix or about chasing the latest trend. It's about following one simple rule: Almost every piece you purchase should have the ability to take on more than one role in your current or future home. We're not suggesting that you move your sofa, bed, or dining-room table from room to room. We're talking about pieces like the small love seat that we bought for Lauren's first apartment. It looks fabulous in her teeny-tiny living room, but one day it will look equally chic in a larger space at the foot of her bed. The night tables in Suzanne's bedroom (a pair of DIY painted tag-sale finds) work just as well as side tables on either side of the living-room sofa. These are the "filler" pieces

that many people find difficult to identify but are essential to creating a soulful, functioning space.

"Furniture pigeonholing," as we like to call it, is a creative buzzkill. A good example of this is buying a big hulking desk to work from at home. That's the definition of an inflexible piece. Just because a table isn't specifically labeled "desk" doesn't mean it can't be used as one. In fact, some of the most interesting desks we've seen use less obvious tabletops (we're writing this on a glass top IKEA dining table).

When it comes to designing spaces that are fresh, as well as economically and

**OPPOSITE AND ABOVE** Finding diamonds in the rough at the Brimfield Antique Show in Brimfield, Massachusetts. Brimfield is a triannual, outdoor antiques show that sets up along a half-mile stretch of Route 20 in May, July, and September.

VOGUE LIVING HOUSES, GARDENS, PEOPLE

ART AT WORK

E. P. DUTTON

So let's get started. Here are the pieces that give a home longevity. They're great pieces with good bones. And they're coming with us wherever we go.

environmentally responsible, you've got to break some rules. The key pieces that make up your home shouldn't be stagnant; they should have the transformative power to be more than just your desk or your dresser. When we talk about being flexible and mobile, we don't mean cheap. Buying a bunch of poor-quality furniture that eventually ends up in a dumpster is wasteful. A wise man once said, "Buy the best and you'll only cry once." Each and every piece you choose should have legs—if you can't see using it again ten years down the road, then it's not worth investing in.

When a great table catches our eye, we think about all the different ways we can use it in multiple locations. This way of thinking is not only practical, it's also a learned technique for creating rooms that always look interesting. Some of your best pieces might already be under your roof, or maybe even your mother's. They're just waiting to be given a fresh start.

# THE LOVE SEAT

---

## WHERE TO USE IT

**STARTER APARTMENT, LIVING ROOM, DINING OR BREAKFAST ROOM, BEDROOM**

$\mathcal{N}$ot to pick favorites, but the love seat is probably our most beloved—no pun intended—multifunctional piece. We are both continuously attracted to its lovely proportions and its ability to "fit in" in almost any room. It's a classic rotatable piece that can be bought for a first apartment as the main seating option, be moved to your next home and paired with a bigger sofa in a larger living room, and it can sit at the foot of your bed once you get that spacious master bedroom you've been waiting for. Love seats are also fantastic when you're working with a large or oddly shaped living room where it's appropriate to create two or more separate seating areas. There's no other sofa capable of taking on quite as many roles as the love seat, and that's why we love it.

The very first love seats were made in the late seventeenth century—one of the first was known as the Knole settee,

There's no other sofa capable of taking on quite as many roles as the love seat, and that's why we love it.

named after its first home, Knole, in Kent, England. In fact, modern reproductions of this piece are still being made today.

There is no right or wrong love seat for any room—because of its smaller dimensions, it is difficult to make a mistake. In fact, the love seat can be a great opportunity to bring in a daring shape or color that you might not want to commit to in a regular-size sofa. But a sofa of any size is always a big investment for your home, so it's important to choose one that is well made. Like any type of seating, you should try out the piece you're considering purchasing. Reupholstering can be expensive, so definitely take time to examine the piece closely to be sure that the basic construction is good. Are the seat cushions the perfect combination of soft down feathers and polyester Dacron? We like 50 percent polyester Dacron, 50 percent down, but this is a matter of personal taste (kind of like choosing the pillows you lay your head on at night). Is the seat cushion deep enough from front to back for you to sink into? Is the seat back pitched slightly backward to allow you to sit comfortably? Well-made love seats can range in price from $1,000 to $5,000 and up. Keep your eye out for sales—if you're going to buy a sofa at a retail store, you should never pay full price. Remember: Furniture goes on sale just like clothing.

In a first apartment, especially in New York City where space is at a premium, there's often only space for a love seat, a coffee table, and a small chair or bench. But just because your space is small doesn't mean you can't create the perfect living area. We see lots of spaces where oversize sofas are crammed into a tiny room, making the space appear even smaller than it is. In the wise words of legendary decorator Dorothy Draper: "A technical knowledge of architecture is not necessary to know that a huge stuffed leather chair in a tiny gold and cream room is . . . as much out of proportion as the proverbial bull in the china shop" (*Decorating Is Fun!*, 1939). For pint-size apartments, less furniture is more, but it's all about scale. Before you go shopping for a love seat, measure the wall in front of which your sofa will be placed. Choose a wall that allows for two side tables at least twenty-two inches wide (each) on either side of the sofa. Including these pieces will ultimately make your love seat more functional. Remember: You don't have to buy a huge sofa just because it's your very first purchase for your very first space. Find a piece that suits the dimensions you're living in now. There will always be a place for the love seat in your future.

A pair of vintage mini Swedish cocktail tables are elegant and unobtrusive in Lauren's small living area. The mustard yellow gourd lamp was a flea-market find.

> "I've always been partial to **love seats** as opposed to big hulking sofas. I love how **delicate** and **inherently romantic** they are."
> —*LAUREN*

Some kind of window treatment was a must to disguise the industrial window guards in this New York City rental. From IKEA, this curtain fabric reminded us of a favorite Victoria Hagan textile.

The most expensive thing we bought for Lauren's first apartment after she graduated from Bowdoin was the love seat (even though it was on sale). We went for the pretty gray ticking stripe because of its neutrality—yes, stripes and patterns can be neutral. What's more, the exposed wood legs have casters on them, making it easy to move the piece around a room. We're big fans of exposed legs on sofas for two reasons: They're easier to clean under than sofas with skirts, and they eliminate the possibility of the dreaded shoe-polish stains from men's and women's boots.

When you're young and constantly moving, love seats make getting up narrow hallways and around tight corners much easier than if you are hauling the average-size sofa. While decorating Lauren's first apartment, we made the mistake of not measuring

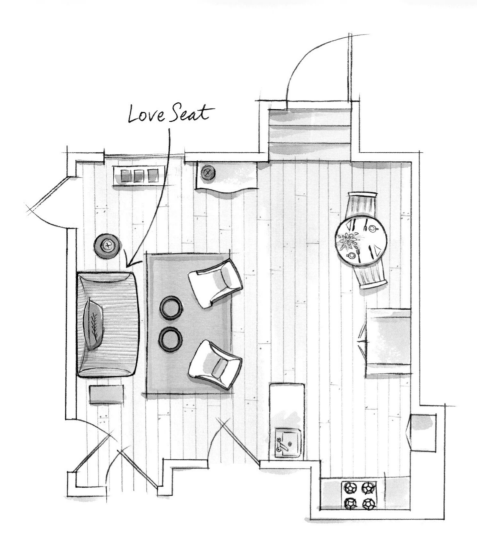

Love Seat

width of the extremely narrow staircase to her new apartment before buying the love seat. On move-in day, after much pushing and pulling, we finally came to terms with the fact that the sofa was not going to make it up to the second floor—not by the stairs, that is. In a stroke of sheer genius—and with the help of her very friendly neighbors—we were able to bring the piece up through the adjacent brownstone and hoist it over the back terrace onto Lauren's. So, word to the wise: Make sure you not only measure the wall your piece will be going against, but also measure the width and height of every door and hallway it has to pass through to get to your apartment.

> "The more you educate yourself about classic forms and historically relevant pieces, the easier it will be to pick out a great 'inspired-by' piece that fits your budget." —*Suzanne*

When decorating first apartments, we're almost always on a tight budget, so we usually spend the most money on the love seat or sofa to ensure that it will endure lots of wear and tear. In the living room of a friend's small apartment in the East Village, we chose an elegant Louis XVI–style love seat with uniquely small dimensions (fifty-one inches in width). This piece is a nice combination of materials with its plush seat cushions and elegant wood frame. Choosing a love seat with such classic lines allowed us to be more daring with some of the other choices we made in the room. One of the first pieces we found, a Lucite-framed reproduction of a Paule Marrot textile, became the launching pad for the space's color scheme. Any classically trained decorator will tell you to commit to a rug before you decide on any of the other elements in a room, but sometimes it's okay to start elsewhere if you're particularly inspired by a certain piece. For this room, the artwork took on the role of the carpet in dictating the colors and tone of the space.

While scrounging around in a local consignment store, we spotted a contemporary Warren Platner for Knoll–inspired coffee table for $175. It had been painted green by its previous owner,

A bright green color reform rug from Stark Carpet brings the outdoors in.

A couple of install-it-yourself shelves from Home Depot provide a place to display some colorful collectibles.

and we thought it provided a nice contrast to the traditional form of the love seat. This piece may not have cost a lot, but it adds so much to the space. To get around making the living area feel too table heavy, we chose a modern brass standing lamp for one side of the love seat.

In this apartment, there wasn't room for even a small chair without making the pint-size living room look jam-packed with furniture. To avoid this, we found an elegant tufted mid-century-modern bench with bamboo-style painted legs that seamlessly fits below the built-in bookshelves. Here, the bench takes up very little floor space while providing double the seating in this tiny alcove. This piece was a wonderful addition to the living space because two can sit on it comfortably when there's company, and when it's not in use, it can be tucked right under the bookshelves to maximize the usable space.

# REUPHOLSTERING A SOFA

We like to re-cover sofas once the fabric starts to fade, but it's also nice to do it when you want to change the overall feel of a room. Upholstering a sofa is no easy task, and it's best left to professionals. Ask to see samples of reupholstered pieces or visit the workroom of the upholsterer you're consider working with. If you decide to invest in re-covering an old sofa, it's a good idea to refill or, if necessary, replace the seat cushions. This way, not only will your refurbished piece look good, it will feel good as well. If you'd rather purchase a new piece, you'll find that many retail furniture stores offer different in-house fabric options for upholstering their pieces. Alternatively, if you see COM (Customer's Own Material) displayed anywhere, the retailer allows you to use your own fabric instead of the one supplied by the furniture store. This is a great way to get a well-made, quality-guaranteed piece from a retailer with a more custom result.

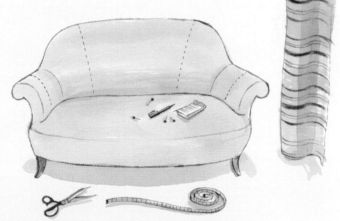

**1 DO YOUR HOMEWORK** Verify the exact quantity of fabric you'll need with your upholsterer before you purchase. You don't want to buy more fabric than you need.

**2 CHOOSE THE RIGHT FABRIC** Use an upholstery-weight, unfussy fabric. This is the key to a long-lasting upholstered piece.

**3 CHECK THE FABRIC WEARABILITY CODE** (the industry's guidelines for determining the strength and best use for a fabric). The higher the number of "double rubs" a fabric can sustain, the more durable it is. More than 15,000 double rubs classifies a fabric as heavy duty.

"My first sofa from twenty-five years ago still has a prominent place in my living room. It was originally covered in a pink woven fabric, then a wonderful cotton maize, then a shiny blood-red glazed chintz, and now it's re-covered in a creamy white glazed cotton. It's the piece in my home that's been reincarnated the most." —Suzanne

Moving to a bigger space? The love seat acts as a great balancing piece in a larger living room where more seating options are necessary. In our house in Rye, New York, we created an intimate place for family and friends to gather by pairing a larger sofa with a small love seat. The curved tight-back French-style love seat, found at a closeout sale of custom upholstery, is covered in a white glazed cotton that makes it one of the most heavily rotated pieces in the house. This sofa has lived just about everywhere because of its neutral color, clean lines, and accommodating size.

One strategy when designing large rooms like this one is to keep all of the upholstered pieces in neutral, complementary colors and then add color with accessories like pillows, throws, rugs, and

When the upholstered pieces are neutral, it's easy to mix and match pillows. The zig-zag rug is Madeline Weinrib.

> "Start by putting more objects than you think you need on the shelves, then step back and edit. If you want to **mix your collectibles in with books,** try to stay away from placing pairs of things—such as **vases or bookends**—next to each other. This will help to keep your shelves from looking forced." —*LAUREN*

artwork. At the back of the room are two built-in bookshelves that present another opportunity to add color. Edith Wharton wrote in her 1897 book, *The Decoration of Houses*, "Those who really care for books are seldom content to restrict them to the library, for nothing adds more to the charm of a drawing room than a well-designed bookcase: an expanse of beautiful bindings is as decorative as a fine tapestry." We like to organize books— some vertically and others horizontally—with the largest books stacked horizontally at the bottom of the bookcase. Including a collection of interesting objects—ceramic pieces or wicker baskets or framed prints—adds an eclectic feel.

In this New York City apartment decorated by color-confident interior designer Miles Redd, a vibrant sapphire satin upholstered camelback love seat helps to create a seating area that is separate from the main one. This can be an especially effective technique when you're working with an oddly shaped room. "We didn't want the typical circle-around-the-fireplace plan in this long,

The parrot green de Gournay wallpaper makes the perfect backdrop for a pair of hot pink French Bergere chairs.

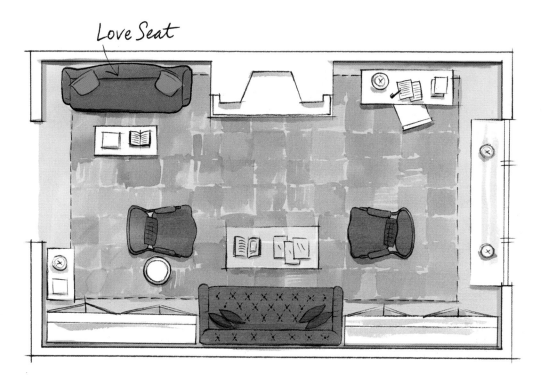

Love Seat

**ABOVE** Miles Redd's floor plan created a cozy nook for the camelback love seat to live. **OPPOSITE** Redd fused modern and classical, hanging an Ellsworth Kelly lithograph on top of the hand-painted de Gournay wall covering.

skinny room," explains Redd. "Putting the sofa here at one side of the fireplace created a nook outside the hallway, but within the living room, for guests to perch on during cocktail parties. The homeowner loves to entertain and has a very doors-wide-open sensibility, so it was nice to have another seating area in the room without ruining the flow of the space."

The small-scale coffee table in front of the love seat is a perfect illustration of a balanced pairing of sofa and coffee table. As a general rule, the coffee table in front of your sofa should be slightly lower than your sofa, at a height of about twelve inches above the floor. This coffee table was a piece that Redd had not planned on including originally, but fell in love with as the project evolved. "I'm a big believer in having a floor plan; but great objects are what make a room beautiful rather than a very rigid map," explains Redd. "You have to be flexible if you find a piece you fall in love with."

**OPPOSITE** Hanging art on a bookshelf is an unexpected way to display a favorite painting or photograph. **ABOVE** The round gold and black mirror adds a new shape into the room.

# PILLOW STYLING

## Do:

Play with color and pattern.

If the proportions are right,
stripes, florals, and animal print
can all share the spotlight.

## Don't:

Don't be matchy-matchy!

Using the same fabric for
your window treatments and the
pillows on your sofa is humdrum.

Pillows are every decorator's go-to accessory. They can act as the finishing touch on a well-designed room or truly transform a blank-slate space. Accessorizing with pillows is an easy way to change the look of a room without breaking the bank, especially when things start to feel a bit stale.

## A FEW TIPS

1 **BANG FOR YOUR BUCK.** Pillows present a great opportunity to add a new texture or lux fabric into the mix. You may not be able to afford to upholster a large furniture piece in your fabric of choice, but you could certainly have a few special pillows made out of it.

2 **ASYMMETRY IS THE NAME OF THE GAME.** Place two pillows on one end of the sofa and one at the other. Using odd numbers of objects is a good general rule for accessorizing.

3 **BIGGER ISN'T ALWAYS BETTER.** Anything larger than twenty-four by twenty-four inches is probably going to overpower a sofa, especially a love seat.

4 **LESS IS MORE.** More than five pillows on a regular-size sofa or more than two on a love seat starts to make the piece look overcrowded.

"**Far too often when my husband goes out to the movies with our son,** he'll come back two hours later, and **Lauren and I will have moved everything around the house.**" —*Suzanne*

In our house, we placed a pair of matching love seats (though they certainly don't have to match to work!) facing each other on either side of the fireplace. It's rare to find a pair of antique or vintage love seats, but when you do, it's a great excuse to create a living space around them. A small black and gold coffee table found at a consignment store is the perfect size to go in between. A pair of love seats also look chic pushed up against the walls on either side of a fireplace or on either side of a wide entranceway. When you have a pair, it's nice to have the option of setting them across from each other (as we have) or splitting them up and putting one in another room of your home. As you can see, there certainly isn't a shortage of places to put one.

The wood stool was found at the Salvation Army. We "reupholstered" it by stapling some leftover Brunschwig & Fils ikat to the seat cushion. The color reform rug is from ABC Carpet & Home. The antique Italian sconces above the mantel were purchased at the Pier Show in New York City. They were missing a few of their crystals, so we were able to bargain with the dealer. For us, these sconces make a bold statement even if they aren't in perfect condition.

A love seat in the bedroom is a great spot to read a book, drink your morning coffee, put on your shoes, or drape your clothes over for the next day.

We're always moving furniture around the house to create new arrangements with what we already have. So, when we've grown tired of using our pair of love seats in the living room, we'll bring one upstairs to the master bedroom and totally reconfigure the living room. The side tables on either side of the bed were found at a thrift store. We were initially attracted to their unique curved legs; it wasn't until we brought them home and inspected them that we realized they were made by Kroehler, a now defunct but once quite reputable American furniture maker. A couple of coats of BEHR Castle Path high-gloss paint later, our pair of side tables looked instantly modern and fresh. We chose to preserve the solid brass hardware, but changing out the hardware on an old piece can be a great way to give it a little extra personality.

**OPPOSITE** The Swedish loom-woven rug was a ten-dollar Brimfield find. The camelback love seat is John Derian for Cisco Brothers.

The mini love seat at the foot of this five-year-old girl's bed was found by Miles Redd at an auction. He decided to leave the bright green upholstery because it was such a beautiful color. When these miniature furniture pieces turn up at house auctions and estate sales, they are always highly sought after because it's so difficult to find well-made upholstered children's furniture today. The zebra wallpaper is an archival Scalamandré print introduced in the 1940s; it was on the walls of the homeowner's favorite childhood restaurant, Gino (now closed), on the Upper East Side.

The Charles P. Rogers canapé bed is left unadorned, letting the striking Scalamandré wallpaper take center stage.

The exotic, hand-painted Zuber wall covering in the foyer dictated the serene, neutral colors in the rest of the apartment.

When we designed the dining room of this New York apartment, we knew that our client's post-college daughters would be living in it while working and attending graduate school so we wanted to create a space conducive to lots of fun dinner parties. The best recipe for a functional entertaining space is lots of seating. With eight chairs around the oval table, as well as this chic armless love seat, there's plenty of room for everyone. The settee is upholstered in an elegant damask (an ode to Fortuny but at a better price point) while the graphic, Greek-key pillows give the piece a modern edge.

Although the color scheme of the apartment is quite sedate, we took every opportunity to layer tints and shades of the predominant colors of beige, caramel, and brown. On the walls in the dining room, we chose an intense Farrow & Ball bisquit beige called Clunch, paired with our favorite creamy white Benjamin Moore trim color, Ivory White. To draw the eye up and highlight the architectural elements of the room, we painted the space between the cornice molding and ceiling Benjamin Moore Pale Oak. This is a great trick to make rooms feel bigger, and the ceilings higher.

# LOVE SEAT
# GLOSSARY

When shopping for love seats, we tend to favor ones with a tight back. Too many loose cushions on a small sofa can look messy. The standard Louis XVI–style love seat is a foolproof form that looks good pretty much everywhere, while the reverse camelback (F) helps bring a new and unexpected shape into any room. The Bridgewater (D) is one of the most comfortable love-seat styles, as they are usually fairly deep. You can find some of the best love seats at antique warehouses, where they've often come from a custom upholstery shop or are one-offs designed by interior decorators. These are great pieces because they're well made but also unique.

A

B

C

D

E

F

G

H

I

**A** Lee Jofa  **B** Design Within Reach  **C** 1stdibs  **D** Lee Industries
**E** Country Swedish  **F** John Derian for Cisco Brothers  **G** Jonathan
Adler  **H** Crate & Barrel  **I** Jayson Home & Garden

# 2

# THE DEMILUNE

---

## WHERE TO USE IT

ENTRANCE FOYER, STARTER APARTMENT, LIVING ROOM,
STAIRCASE LANDING, HOME OFFICE, BEDROOM

$\mathcal{I}$t's rare to find someone outside the design world who knows what a demilune table is. "The demi-what?" is the most common response when we bring it up. Despite its lack of name recognition, this sophisticated piece of furniture has had a long and important role in the history of decorative arts. The demilune, French for "half-moon," is a beautifully sculptural piece; but don't let its delicacy fool you, this table works hard in just about any room of the house. Whether as a pair or a single, the demilune takes you where your average table doesn't.

We love to use a pair of demilunes in the traditional style, flanking the sides of a fireplace or on either side of a doorway. However, when there is only a single, the demilune works in the foyer as a space-efficient entrance-hall table or in a small apartment as an eat-in-kitchen table. We've even used it as a vanity.

When shopping for vintage and antique demilune tables, it's unusual to find a pair. Over time, the two halves were often separated within families, so if you find two demilunes that are original to each other, you've done well.

Occasionally, you'll come across tables that were designed to be fastened together underneath to make a round table; when not in use, they were unhooked and pushed up against the wall. These are the most appealing because they're truly multifunctional.

Something you want to take into account when collecting furniture pieces for your home is assembling an assortment of different shapes. A room filled with only square and rectangular pieces is not an interesting space. The most successful rooms are furnished with a mix of circles, squares, and rectangles. The demilune will always be a nice balancing piece in a room where there are pieces of different sizes, shapes, and proportions. The simplicity in their design makes them a welcome addition to many of the eclectic rooms we admire. From the eat-in-kitchen table of your first apartment to the statement piece on your stairway landing, this table delivers.

"It's a lot more work to find diamonds in the rough, but you'll love the pieces you acquire from 'unedited' places more because you'll feel like you discovered them." —*Suzanne*

We're firm believers in making a good first impression—which is why it's so important to make the entryway beautiful. We found this Swedish demilune table at an antiques warehouse in Connecticut. It's not in perfect condition—and its mate is long gone—but we loved it immediately because it was such a wonderful shade of weathered gray. A glam gilded mirror hangs above it while a collection of vintage egg prints in shades of blue and gray are assembled below to add another layer of interest to the vignette.

Aside from adding an element of Swedish design to the foyer of our home, this demilune table also creates room for a much needed table lamp. Hallways in older homes and apartments are often dark and lack recessed lighting or even a ceiling fixture. We love the romantic look of this table when the lamp is turned on. The balance of the elegant half-round table with the primitive American dotted-clay lamp is an example of how two pieces from different time periods and countries can come together and look like they were made for each other.

"What paint color are your foyer walls?" is perhaps one of the most common questions we get from our blog readers. It's our all-time favorite blue, DKC-29 by Donald Kaufman.

Without the space for a proper table, many first-time apartment dwellers end up eating the majority of their meals on the couch. One way to make this experience a little more civilized is to use the demilune. Taking up half the space of a traditional kitchen table, it becomes an investment piece that you won't trash when you make your next move.

In this New York City apartment, the living room is the dining room and the kitchen all in one. A demilune table was the perfect solution to create a place for this twenty-something to sit and eat a quick breakfast before she dashes off to work. It's also a makeshift desk for when she needs to work from home. We love mixing old and new, modern and traditional together, and wanted to find a pair of chairs that could be juxtaposed with the traditional lines of this Swedish demilune. We found our match when we came across these Lucite ballroom chairs at a consignment store. Lucite furniture is one of our secret weapons; its transparent quality combats the clutter factor of small spaces. With the seat cushions re-covered in a fresh leopard print, the chairs add a modern edge to the room.

OPPOSITE A wall of mismatched illustrations and photographs gives this space a homey, lived-in feeling. ABOVE Painting the inside of your kitchen shelves is a great way to add a shot of color.

In the narrow entryway of this New York City apartment, this simple Chinese-style bamboo demilune table literally hugs the wall. Its round edges make it the perfect piece for this busy thoroughfare where three small children are constantly coming and going. Tricycles and scooters move through this hallway with ease. The demilune table's lack of flow-disrupting sharp corners is part of why it's so often found in foyers and entryways. Most other tables tend to obstruct one of the most used passageways in the home. A bright-green Chinese vase gives the neutral hallway a pop of color and serves as the ideal vessel for a tall arrangement of cherry blossoms. Every entryway needs a place to drop daily mail, newspapers, and keys. Why not let the demilune serve that role?

The cork-lined walls, a signature Miles Redd detail, are a chic and unexpected choice in this sophisticated entryway.

Decorating is truly a process, and one thing really does lead to another. The more flexible you are, the more interesting your rooms will be. Even though it's important to make a furniture plan, you still want to leave room for unexpected finds. In the case of this classic-six apartment, we had a furniture plan before we got started, but we left placeholders for what would go on either side of the fireplace. One morning, while visiting one of our favorite furniture dealers, we happened upon a delicate pair of demilune tables that immediately filled in the blank. Their soft hue and simple lines help make an otherwise formal room more accessible. What's more, this pair of demilune tables on either side of the mantel allow for extra lighting as well as an opportunity to hang art or mirrors above.

The starting point for this room, in terms of color, came from the dramatic Zuber wall covering in the foyer (see page 55)—something our client had inherited from the previous owner. To complement the colorful entryway, we painted the living-room walls a dressy silver-gray (Pale Oak, OC-20, from Benjamin Moore). We wanted to keep the palette neutral so as not to compete with the elaborate wall covering in the adjacent room. Above the Swedish demilunes hang a pair of bold abstract paintings. We left

A pair of antique Swedish demilune tables flank the fireplace, stabilizing the seating arrangements and lending a nice symmetry to the room.

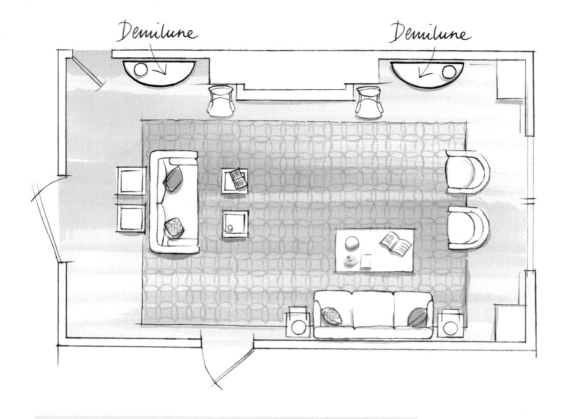

Demilune    Demilune

ABOVE The living room's floor plan. OPPOSITE The new metallic gourd lamp with lucite base and bold abstract art give the delicate demilune some kick.

them unframed to keep the space feeling casual and unfussy. Whenever you're decorating a room, keep in mind that there is great beauty in furniture pieces that are old, even if they're slightly damaged or distressed. They add an element of history and character to a home that you just can't replicate with a room full of new furniture.

The mantelpiece, and how you style it, is as important as which sofa or club chairs you choose (see page 73). Oftentimes this space

above the fireplace is neglected or, on the flip side, cluttered with too many little knickknacks. The scale of objects placed on the mantel is vital; here, bigger is better. There's no greater eyesore than a mantel full of objects that are just too small. Another thing: This is not the place to display all of your family photographs. Try a few stylized prints or artistic photographs leaned against the mirror or wall instead.

The mantelpiece in this New York City apartment is simple and shows the transformative

power of flowers. Just a few branches placed in a pretty glass vessel add both height and a lovely sculptural element to this simple mantel. We like to choose at least one or often two pieces that are really large (and this can include wall sconces). When you place your objects, try to follow the architectural lines of the fireplace itself. This mantel has columns, so we stood a pair of tall candlesticks above them. Artwork over a mantelpiece works (if you've got it), but mirrors are best because they reflect light and can add interesting perspective to a room.

**LEFT** A foolproof window treatment for even the most urban windows is to combine elegant, neutral textiles with tailored Paris pleat panels and simple unlined roman shades. All textiles are Rogers & Goffigon. **ABOVE** A well-appointed mantel includes accessories of varying shapes and heights and isn't overly symmetrical.

"This pin board was created using a tag-sale vintage frame, a large piece of foam core, and some burlap—a chic alternative to the traditional bulletin board."
— LAUREN

In one of the corners of this master bedroom in Suzanne's home, we created a small at-home office using a modern lacquered demilune. This very feminine piece works well in a room where a traditional desk might take over or clutter the space. It can also play vanity when it's not being used as a desk as its front legs are wide enough apart that you can comfortably swing your feet underneath.

For us, mixing new and old is what defines great style. This vintage Italian occasional chair is the perfect complement to a new, lacquered demilune table by Oomph.

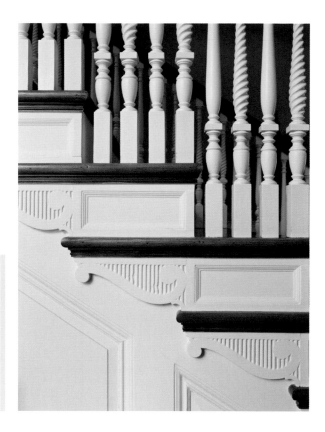

**OPPOSITE** The staircase in this late-Georgian-style home is an architectural gem. We didn't want anything too obtrusive or overly dramatic on the landing; the demilune felt organic here. **RIGHT** Every spindle and molding detail was hand carved almost one hundred years ago.

In this grand late-Georgian-style home, the demilune table is the focal point as you make your way up the pristine staircase—another important passageway of the home. The unobtrusive demilune brings an interesting decorative element to a very architectural transition space without getting in the way. Not everyone has a landing in their home as magnificent as this one, but this setup illustrates how well the half-circle shape can fill a relatively empty wall and help it look finished. The late nineteenth-century French gilded mirror above the table has some imperfections from wear, but its flaws are almost imperceptible, especially at its height on the wall. This piece is a good example of an antique that is not in perfect condition, but that is still capable of bringing a feeling of grandness and integrity at a reduced price point.

This master bedroom is divided into two rooms, the bedroom and the ante-room, by a small entryway of sorts. A walnut spool-leg demilune purchased by the home-owners is the first piece you see as you walk through the master bedroom door. Robert Indiana's iconic "Love" silkscreen created a nice juxtaposition to the traditional lines of the demilune, as well as a fitting tribute to the couple who live here. At the end of the day, the most successful rooms have a way of revealing something personal about the owners.

Pairing coordinating, but not matching, textile patterns from Brunschwig & Fils' archive collection gives the vintage English chairs and ottoman a more relaxed feel. The lucite cocktail table brings in an element of modernity without overpowering.

# DEMILUNE
## GLOSSARY

There are many different styles of demilune tables. With a wide range of retail stores stocking them in sleek, modern iterations, it's become easier and easier to find one to fit your personal style. We tend to favor Swedish demilune tables (B) because we love their subtle gray-wash painted wood and delicate features, but there are many beautiful French and English demilunes made of handsome woods such as mahogany and walnut. When choosing antiques and decorating on a budget, it's impossible to be a perfectionist. Sometimes it makes sense economically to buy a less-than-pristine piece with a small flaw or inconsistency to get the look you want. Trust us, no one will notice but you.

A

B

C

**D** Kindel  **E** Oly

**F** Oomph  **G** Country Swedish

**A** Zentique  **B** 1stdibs  **C** Lee Jofa  **D** Kindel  **E** Oly  **F** Oomph
**G** Country Swedish  **H** 1stdibs  **I** Keno Brothers

# THE BENCH

## WHERE TO USE IT

FRONT PORCH, ENTRANCE FOYER, LIVING ROOM,
DINING ROOM, BEDROOM

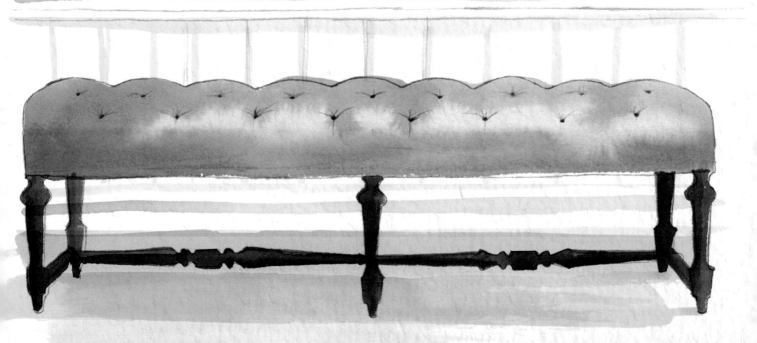

*T*he bench is the unsung hero of many furniture plans. It can add character, color, sculpture, and, most important, extra seating without overwhelming a space. Ready and waiting when the inevitable moment arises when you've got to squeeze in eight guests at a table for six, the bench is an important piece to have in your home's furniture "tool box." Stationed along a long wall in the foyer, the bench serves as a place to take off your shoes and put down your purse, and it's the perfect foot-of-the-bed piece to give a bedroom a more layered, finished look.

While the bench has become one of the most rotatable pieces in the house today, up until the early sixteenth century, it was often an extension of the architecture of homes' interiors. A popular piece during the Middle Ages, it was found in the medieval hall, used as seating during the day but wide enough to be a bed at night. Since then, many beautiful

Upholstering a bench in a vibrant stripe or a bold geometric pattern is an easy way to bring a new pattern or a strong color into a room without taking too much of a risk.

stand-alone benches have been made. Sadly, many homes being built today are reverting back to "fitted furniture," taking away from the art of furniture arrangement and collecting that gives your home its personality and flair. Don't take the easy way out with a boring built-in. Remember: You can't take a built-in with you!

A few years back, we fell in love with a weathered painted bench that originally came from a farm in Ohio and was displayed at the Pier Antiques Show in New York City (see page 88). We were told it had probably lived outside on a porch for most of its life—the distressed wood and charming chipped white paint confirmed this. We loved that it had its own history. In the summer months, you'll find it out on our small front porch, where we gather for coffee on weekend mornings and for cocktails with neighbors and friends later in the day. Once the cold weather arrives, we bring it inside, where it becomes the perfect spot to seat guests during the holiday season.

In this Manhattan apartment, a French Louis XV–style bench is upholstered in a subtle gray leather. As a piece, the bench, with its slender form and unobtrusive style, lends itself well to the narrow hallways and small-scale foyers of city apartments. This serene foyer, designed by Miles Redd, features painted floors with a multicolor concentric-square pattern and cork-covered walls. The large, contemporary framed photograph contrasts with the traditional legs of the bench. In this colorful apartment (see page 41), the neutral foyer acts like a palette cleanser from one strong-colored room to the next.

A great way to add interest to your floors without breaking the bank is to paint them. "I love painted floors in entrance-ways," says Redd. "They're easy to keep clean and give the illusion of a more expansive space." Painted floors are washable and resistant to red-wine stains, while that pricey carpet takes a beating from kids, pets, and dinner-party guests. A solid-color high-gloss-finish paint job is an easy do-it-yourself project.

The Hinson & Company bench is a reproduction of a classic French form made even chicer by the pairing of the work of up-and-coming photographer H.G. Esch.

We fell in love with this weathered painted bench, which originally came from a farm in Ohio, while at the Pier Antiques Show in New York City a few years back.

This is the Ohio farm bench that stands on our mini porch during the summer months. We had a seat cushion upholstered with a durable stripe fabric to make the hard wood more comfortable to sit on. Suzanne's dream has always been to have a house with a wraparound or screened-in porch. While our current house doesn't have either, it does have an elevated landing that we've turned into our own little porch. A few years ago, we covered the floor with wood supplied by a boat manufacturer and finished it with a shiny high-gloss coating that looks great all year round. We made the most of this outdoor space by furnishing it with this primitive bench and a small rattan cube. When the weather is warm, it's everyone's favorite hangout.

Here is the bench from the front porch moved into the main living room. Living rooms always need flexible seating options, so creating many different conversation centers is essential. If you have a relatively large room, it's nice to be able to have a furniture plan that allows for more than one seating area. Enter the bench! Its elegant lines and slender form allow it to fit in to any nook or cranny in your room. Pushed up against a wall or underneath a windowsill—even as a room divider in a long rectangular space—the bench fits discreetly into the living room while offering seating for a few more guests.

An ABC Carpet & Home color reform rug brings a shot of green into the living room. A pair of Oly cupboards in a muted drabware color display Suzanne's ever-growing collection of ironstone pottery.

"Entertaining at home is something we enjoy doing, and the more guests the better. Having a bench to pull up to the table is a necessity." —*Suzanne*

When we have more guests to dinner than our set of six chairs can hold, we'll often pull up the bench that usually rests against one of the walls in the dining room. While traditionalists might gasp at the thought of seating dinner guests on anything but a chair, seating people this way is more informal—and it harks back to one of the bench's original uses during the Middle Ages in Europe. It lets your guests get to know one another—whether they like it or not!

The chandelier above the table was acquired at auction on Nantucket many summers ago. We like the fact that many of the pieces we have collected over the years bring back memories of when and where we found them. The caned-seat chairs surrounding our dining-room table are part of a set we found lined up on the grass in front of a consignment store one Saturday morning. They'd come out of a well-maintained home, most likely from an estate, and still had a tag under the seat identifying them as coming from an important furniture designer in Brazil. We were thrilled to find them—especially because we paid only $300 for the lot.

The wallpaper in our dining room is called Swan Lake by Nina Campbell. The seat cushions of the chairs are covered in Gem Drop by Fabricut, one of our favorite textile makers.

Whenever we have parties, setting the table is as important to us as the menu. Creating interesting table settings is all about layering one element on top of another. OPPOSITE (BOTTOM) Here, we started with round Dransfield & Ross place mats, followed by an ornamental doily to help cut the formality and add a shot of color. Next, we paired two reclaimed patterns of Limoges plates found one summer in Hudson, New York. The D & R pale pink napkins tied with some simple white grosgrain ribbon give the setting its final flourish.

Dining-room sets with matching chairs and table are a dead giveaway that you haven't got a clue (that is, unless you own a very important period table and chairs). An eclectic mix of different styles or eras of table and chairs is a classic decorator's trick. Combining upholstered or slipcovered chairs always looks chic with a glass dining-room table, while painted or wicker chairs are a nice complement to a traditional wood table. When it comes to dining-room tables, square rooms look best with round or oval-shaped tables and more rectilinear chairs. A long rectangular room takes a rectangular table and rounded or balloon-back chairs well. Dining chairs make great occasional chairs too. Pull them away from the table. Move one up to the study, two into your foyer, and another one into your living room.

**OPPOSITE** The gray-washed wood bench is a reproduction Louis XVI found at Restoration Hardware, re-covered in an ikat by Fabricut. The bed linens are by Designer's Guild. **RIGHT** The vintage Venetian-glass mirror was bought at an auction of the contents of an heiress's Fifth Avenue apartment.

We're often asked how to make bedrooms feel less like just a bed floating in the middle of the room with two side tables. Adding a bench is a great way to pull a bedroom together, especially when you're short on space. Not everyone has the square footage in his or her bedroom for a separate seating area, so the bench is a nice alternative that still makes your space feel polished.

We found this simple Louis XVI–style bench on sale at Restoration Hardware and had it re-covered to complement the soothing gray tones of this master bedroom. There's just enough room at the foot of this bed for a light and airy piece such as this one. The side tables on either side of the bed are elegant French neoclassical reproductions that we custom-colored with a glamorous silver-leaf finish (see Side Table Glossary H, page 163).

# DECORATING THE WALL ABOVE THE BED

The question of what to put over the bed is everyone's decorating conundrum. For starters, get a headboard; it sets the stage for a finished bed and whatever you decide to put above it. Our favorite style is this classic, tufted-back rectangle with curved corners and contrast piping (opposite). There are a few configurations that we always return to that help turn this no-man's-land into a chic and well-accessorized wall. From an over-the-top collection of vintage deer antlers to a concave sunburst mirror, here are some foolproof ways to give your bedroom the character and personality it deserves.

**ABOVE LEFT** Designer Lien Luu covers one wall of her serene bedroom with a framed piece of Moroccan embroidery and the other with a small mirror and a pair of prints. **ABOVE RIGHT** A set of four vintage *House & Garden* magazine covers hangs above Lauren's bed in Brooklyn.

## An over-the-top collection

## A series of three prints

## A concave mirror

## One showstopper

## Wallpaper

# BENCH
# GLOSSARY

Some of our favorite styles of benches are classical French Louis XV, simple mid-century modern, painted American, and ultramodern Florence Knoll. We find the most flexible ones to be between approximately thirty-six and sixty-six inches wide. Many have upholstered seat cushions, but you can also have seat cushions made for just about any bench. Upholstering a bench in a vibrant stripe or a bold geometric pattern is an easy way to bring a new pattern or a strong color into a room without taking too much of a risk. Setting a pattern of wide stripes vertically across a seat cushion of any bench is perpetually chic.

A

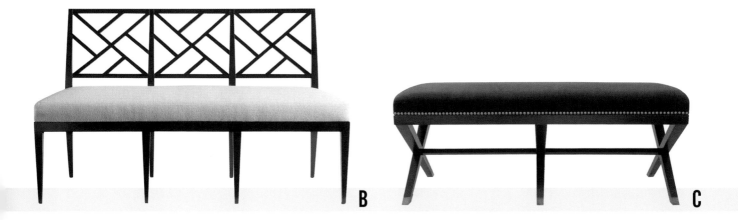

B

C

A **1stdibs**  B **Bolier**  C **Victoria Hagan Home**  D **Design Within Reach**
E **Red Egg**  F **Schumacher**  G **Julian Chichester**  H **Selamat Designs**
I **Suzanne Kasler for Hickory Chair**

# THE DRESSER

---

## WHERE TO USE IT

### ENTRANCE FOYER, LIVING ROOM, DINING ROOM, HALLWAY, BEDROOM, BATHROOM

*T*he dresser is a must-have in any room, and it shouldn't be limited to its conventional spot in the bedroom. We say: Take the dresser out of the bedroom! For centuries, what we today call the dresser, or chest of drawers, has been considered an essential piece of furniture for any household. Manufactured all over the world, some of the finest pieces came from England, France, Scandinavia, and, of course, here in America. "Dressing chest" was a term first used in 1803 by London furniture designer Thomas Chippendale Junior to describe a chest with four drawers, the top one divided into sections to hold dressing accessories.

When people buy a dresser, they often forget to measure the space it will live in, and they don't take into account how difficult it will be to move around. Try not to buy a dresser that is so heavy you'll break your back (and your partner's!) in the event that you need to move it—and trust us, after reading this chapter, you will!

The dresser is a wonderful family heirloom piece. Start your own family tradition by purchasing a piece with good bones that you can pass down to your children and beyond.

The dresser will always look right in the bedroom, but it can also add character and useful storage—as well as another surface to put things on—in the dining room, living room, foyer, or even in a large bathroom. We've found that the most versatile dresser is one with three or four drawers and that is no higher than thirty-six inches and no wider than fifty inches, though a taller dresser can take on many of the same functions. If you own a pair of low dressers—campaign style perhaps—they can look fantastic pushed together against a living-room or entranceway wall with a pair of lamps and a mirror hanging above. Or how about in your dining room as a place to set up coffee and dessert or put a makeshift bar on during a cocktail party? There are so many clever ways to use this fabulous storage piece.

# ACCESSORIZING A VANITY

**1** Add an old-world feel. We like to use vintage pharmacy bottles and fill them with everyday lotions and other bath-and-beauty essentials that often come in not-so-attractive packaging.

**2** An interesting mirror is a must—and represents an opportunity for you to choose something a little more feminine and whimsical than some of the other mirrors in your home. The mirror is the focal point of the vignette, so make sure to choose something with character.

**3** Don't forget your sense of humor! We often find former commercial pieces such as old mannequin hands at flea markets—the perfect objets d'art to display all of your favorite necklaces and rings on (see page 31).

The owner's mahogany dresser had moved here from another room. The small chair has been passed down in their family for generations. A small room like this guest bedroom takes a bold wallpaper by Hines well.

In its most popular role, the dresser is used in the bedroom as a place to store clothing. A dresser doesn't have to be a family heirloom to have good bones, but it's important to choose one that you love the look of, since it isn't a piece you're likely to replace, particularly since it can serve so many purposes. There isn't room in this bedroom for a vanity table, so we created one using the surface of the dresser. All of the necessary pieces—perfumes, makeup, jewelry—fit on top of this hearty piece. Above hangs an utterly romantic white and gold shell-form mirror, which we found partially buried in an antiques emporium.

At one time or another, you've probably been offered a piece of family furniture to "start you out" in your first apartment or home. In Lauren's first apartment, this piece was a dresser that came from her great-grandparents' wedding trousseau; this sounds quite fancy, but it was just part of a three-piece set they were given at the time of their marriage. While three-piece furniture sets today are usually synonymous with poor quality, back then, these pieces were made to last. Since Lauren's bedroom was only large enough for a full-size bed and a small table—and, after all, putting the dresser in the bedroom would be far too ordinary (wink)—we brought it into the living room as a place to store everything from table linens and towels to sweaters and jeans. Originally stained wood, it was modernized with a coat of paint (Elephant Tusk, OC-8, from Benjamin Moore) and a new set of knobs on the top drawer.

**OPPOSITE** The headboard is covered in a Studio Bon ricrac textile. The linens and rug are by John Robshaw.

Sometimes when space is at a premium and you don't have the luxury of having two night tables on either side of your bed or more than one tabletop in the room, the dresser comes to the rescue as a night table–cum–storage. In a small apartment it allows for extra storage as well as providing a flat surface for a light source, an alarm clock, and all the books or magazines you're currently reading. The dresser in this children's room is a midcentury modern piece that fits perfectly in the space between the bed and the window. With all the wear and tear that kids' rooms endure, it can be hard to justify putting nice furniture in their bedrooms. In the end, though, purchasing pieces that your child won't outgrow is more economical. If you buy pieces that are well-made and unfussy, they'll outlast any kiddie furniture in style and substance.

In a kid's room, it's fun to play with pattern and color. We mixed a graphic navy blue ricrac headboard and striped bedskirt with a geometric cotton dhurrie. Above the bed hangs a collection of antlers culled from various antique shows and flea markets.

In a larger bedroom, we like the look of a single dresser on one side of the bed paired with a contrasting piece such as a round pedestal table. Bedrooms are often highly symmetrical, so it's nice to throw things off a little with two different bedside "tables." Ideally, they are the same height on both sides or very close. In an especially large room with a large bed, two small-scale dressers on either side will often look much better than a traditional pair of smaller side tables. In this master bedroom, the homeowners wanted to incorporate their very high Caribbean-style bed into the room. For any designer, starting from scratch in a room is always easier; but finding ways to include clients' pieces, which often have sentimental value, is what gives rooms their eclectic feel. Faced with the challenge of finding a bedside table that was tall enough as well as substantial enough to stand up to the grandness of the bed, we found the dresser was the perfect solution. The romantic gray-painted, serpentine chest fills the space next to this unusually high bed well, while at the same time bringing a softness to the space. Hanging above the bed is a collection of six antique coral prints that were found at Brimfield. We had them framed in a silvery finish to complement the gray-wash finish of the dresser.

The crystal Ralph Lauren Home lamp gives this master bedroom a hint of glamour. The obelisks were found at the Harwich Antique Center on Cape Cod.

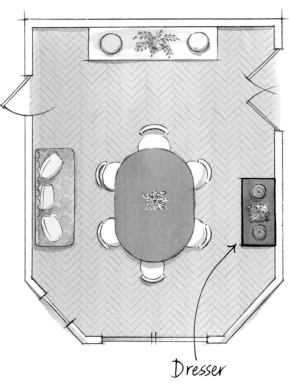

Dresser

A dresser is a great addition to the dining room. And it's nice to use one that has some interesting detail such as a beautiful wood patina or a graphic element. Seeing the unexpected in a room that is typically furnished with a table, a sideboard, and chairs is fun and will definitely give the dining room a feeling of originality. A dresser in the dining room is also practical. It's a place to store table linens and candles, as well as the large bowls, platters, and trays that can make a room feel cluttered if they are left out. In this apartment in New York City, we stationed a classic ebony dresser to the left of the entrance to the dining room. The extra-large mirror that hangs above helps to reflect as much light as possible throughout this naturally shady room, while a pair of brilliantly hued Italian glass lamps bring a shot of color into the otherwise neutral color scheme.

In your living room or family room, the dresser morphs into the perfect bar. One of our favorite examples is in this colorful Miles Redd–decorated apartment. An eye-catching lacquered Hermès-orange Chinese dresser is set up to serve brunch guests a spicy Bloody Mary. This dresser makes the perfect bar for practical reasons, too, because you can store tall bottles and glasses behind the doors on the bottom shelf and napkins and other entertaining necessities in the drawers above.

Above the dresser, a framed abstract work from Josef Albers's *Homage to the Square* series hangs dramatically on top of the bold black-and-white wallpaper, while a pair of black tole odalisque lamps complete the vibrant vignette. The themes of the wallpaper and the art are largely irrelevant. In fact, mixing wallpaper and artwork from different centuries is much more visually appealing than sticking to one time period or the same country of origin.

Designer Miles Redd is a pro at pairing unexpected colors. Here he mixes orange and black without a hint of Halloween.

One of Lien's favorite colors is blue. The walls of her apartment are painted Farrow & Ball Light Blue 22. The light fixture is a garden ornament that Lien turned into a sconce.

Interior designer Lien Luu placed an inexpensive, pale-green painted dresser—a flea-market find—in the foyer of her apartment. Above hangs a Scandinavian walnut mirror with a leather strap that Lien found at the Paris flea market. Her charming hat collection comes from her travels for work in several Caribbean locations including Anguilla, St. Barts, and St. Martin. In any foyer or entrance hall, it's important to have a place to put your keys and mail as well as store your hats, mittens, and scarves if you don't have a mudroom or a large closet nearby. It's probably not a good idea to put a very precious piece of furniture in a hallway or foyer because it will be subjected to plenty of wear and tear from weather, kids, pets, and party guests. For this reason, painted furniture is a great solution here.

Campaign dressers, with their simple, sturdy design and lack of ornamentation, make the perfect pieces to push up next to each other to create a console of sorts. Campaign dressers are a personal favorite of ours and have become popular lately both in retail furniture stores (the original designs having been modified for modern rooms) and in antique or vintage stores. The original campaign dressers were made for officers and nobility during the British military campaigns of the Peninsular War (1808–14) and continued to be manufactured throughout the nineteenth century. Portable and flexible in their design, with sunken brass handles and small feet that could be removed during transport, these pieces have truly stood the test of time.

The simplicity of the campaign dresser makes it a great candidate for a bright paint job. We found this pair of twentieth-century reproductions at the Salvation Army and gave them a few coats of Benjamin Moore's Deep Ocean paint.

# DRESSER GLOSSARY

We find the most versatile dressers to be those with three drawers and with a height of no more than thirty-six inches. Choosing a dresser of this particular size and style will maximize its functionality throughout your home. When we find vintage dressers at flea markets and tag sales that are a little beat up but with good bones, we usually give them a couple of coats of paint. Just because the wood on a found piece isn't perfect, doesn't mean it won't make a great painted piece. There are lots of chic dressers at every price point available in retail stores—look for ones with a striking architectural patina or other special detail.

**A**

**B**

**C**

**A** Williams Sonoma  **B** Kindel  **C** Mecox Gardens  **D** Thomas O'Brien for Hickory Chair  **E** Hickory Chair Atelier  **F** Crate & Barrel  **G** Barbara Barry for Baker  **H** Bernhardt  **I** Nancy Corzine

# THE SLIPPER CHAIR

---

## WHERE TO USE IT

### BEDROOM, LIVING ROOM, FAMILY ROOM, DRESSING ROOM

*M*ade famous by the great American decorator Billy Baldwin, the slipper chair was, up until the 1950s, relegated to the bedroom. Showing up for the first time in eighteenth-century Europe, the slipper chair was originally unupholstered, with a high back, short legs, and a low seat. It was the chair in the bedroom on which women sat to put on their slippers (hence the name) or nurse their babies in the middle of the night. Fast-forward two hundred years to Baldwin's redesign, when the slender chair became boxier, deeper, and fully upholstered. Chic, sleek, and much more comfortable, the now-iconic slipper chair made its way into living rooms, libraries, and foyers all over the world.

The slipper chair is by far the most versatile upholstered chair. It moves seamlessly from room to room, its armless body making it a go-to seating option for small and big spaces alike.

---

The first time Suzanne saw a slipper chair was at her friend Suzie's newlywed apartment in Chelsea, London, in the 1980s. The apartment was on the top floor of a wonderful Victorian mansion that had been broken up into smaller apartments. It had a generous living room with a beautiful marble fireplace mantel and a wall of tall, wide windows. Suzie had an innate sense of style and furnished her living room with a collection of great pieces that she'd found or that had been passed along to her from friends and family; the room was perfectly edited. The magic of that room was Suzie's decision to throw in two Billy Baldwin–style slipper chairs upholstered in a bright pink woven cotton. They were incredibly fresh and modern looking. Suzie still has those slipper chairs, and she's taken them with her wherever she's moved.

"The **slipper chair** in my bedroom at home is the only seating in the room. Admittedly, it often serves as a dependable place to throw yesterday's jeans and sweater, but most of the time it's **my favorite place** to talk on the phone. It's the absolute coziest chair." *—LAUREN*

A modern take on an art deco slipper chair covered in a cheerful Victoria Hagan print fabric sits in Lauren's bedroom in Rye. During a recent update in our living room, the colors in the print fabric of this chair no longer seemed to fit. We brought it up to Lauren's room, where it has become a sweet place to sit and read a book or talk on the phone.

The bright blue mid-century lamp, found at the Rhinebeck Antiques Fair, stands out no matter where we put it in the house.

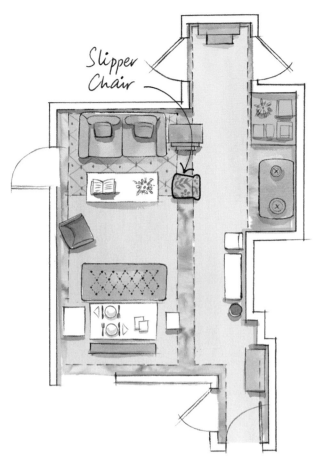

**OPPOSITE** The slipper chair is custom, designed by Luu and covered in a Clarence House velvet. Luu layered a small Moroccan rug over a larger wool sisal. **ABOVE** In a small corner of her living room, Luu created a mini-library for her collection of design and art books.

In her Upper West Side living room, designer Lien Luu chose to include a slipper chair next to her sofa to create the perfect conversation grouping. Her apartment is full of beautiful handpicked pieces; Luu especially likes to mix Scandinavian and Japanese furniture and objects. She found her Scandinavian coffee table at the Paris flea market. "It's very large and higher than a normal coffee table," explains Luu, "which is great for small spaces because it can double as a dining table." The way in which Luu hung the artwork above her sofa is a departure from the typical grid arrangement you often see. She chose to hang a small square next to a large rectangle, and it balances beautifully.

In this large family room, we chose a pair of 1960s Erwin-Lambeth slipper chairs. We were drawn to their curved caned backs and caramel wood that picked up elements of the colors on many of the upholstered pieces. We knew from the outset that this room gets a lot of use, so anything white, neutral, or very dear was out of the question. The space provided an opportunity to have a little fun with strong color and the interplay of patterns.

Creating a room that harmoniously blends many different colors, patterns, and textures can be overwhelming. However, if you understand the basic elements of color theory, you'll find the process a lot less daunting (see page 173).

A mix of prints including ikat, suzani, and stripes dresses up your basic family room. The inlaid bone lamps are from 1stdibs.

Although there are many comfortable places for family members to sit in this New Jersey home, this is the most coveted spot. These low-to-the-ground slipper chairs are reproductions of a French form. The tufted backs and scrolled sides are what make these chairs not your everyday slipper chairs. Re-covered in a hot pink Rose Cummings leopard print linen, these diminutive chairs make a serious statement. Enthusiasts of the Paris flea mar-

ket, the owners had the beautiful marble mantelpiece shipped over from France. There are many architectural-salvage resources across the country (and the world) that rescue stone pieces, statues, urns, sinks, and mirrors from hotels and estates of other eras. These pieces can transform a space, and they are well worth any challenges you might face in getting them into your home.

# SLIPPER CHAIR
# GLOSSARY

We don't recommend buying a piece of furniture just because it looks good, and it's easy to fall into this trap with the slipper chair. There are quite a few slipper chairs out there that are lovely to look at but not in the least bit comfortable. While the slipper chair may be one of the more delicate upholstered chairs, you still want to make sure that the piece you are buying is sturdy. This isn't the chair you'll be curling up in for a Sunday afternoon nap, but it will become one of the most heavily rotated pieces in your home.

A

B

C

D

E

F

G

H

I

**A** McGuire  **B** William Haines  **C** Williams Sonoma  **D** Vaughan  **E** Bolier
**F** Pler One  **G** Victoria Hagan Home  **H** Vanguard  **I** Crate & Barrel

# THE SIDE TABLE

---

**WHERE TO USE IT**

LIVING ROOM, FAMILY ROOM,
BEDROOM, BATHROOM

*T*he side table is both the easiest and the most difficult piece of furniture to shop for.  There are so many options online and in retail stores that pinning down the right ones for your living room, bedroom, library, and everywhere else can be an overwhelming task. The least efficient side tables are those that are too petite and delicate to look proportional anywhere else but in the bedroom. Flexible side tables should be between twenty-four and twenty-six inches tall and have a tabletop large enough to place a lamp, a glass, and a small vase of flowers or an objet d'art.

When it comes to whether side tables should be matching pairs or not—a never-ending debate, it seems—there are no

The good news is that if you choose wisely, the side tables you put on either side of your living-room sofa can also go on either side of the bed, or one can go in between two chairs in your den or even be tucked next to your tub.

hard-and-fast rules. Pairs can add symmetry and balance to a busy room, i.e., one that combines lots of different colors and patterns. However, rooms that feature two side tables that are different from each other can be charming and a little more "undone" looking. If you're going to put nonmatching side tables on either side of a piece of furniture, they don't necessarily have to be the same width (a round pedestal table on one side of the sofa with a rectangular table on the other is a great combo), but they should definitely be the same height (or just about).

A good example of symmetry at work is in this beautiful family room designed by Miles Redd. In a room for young children, a side table with ample storage space is always an asset. Board games, books, and small toys all have a place to go when it's time to clean up, but they're easy for kids to pull out when mom's got her hands full. An oversize photograph by German photographer Elger Esser hangs above this extra-long tufted sofa covered in a durable wool herringbone. All eyes are drawn to the ethereal artwork and shiny lacquered turquoise walls. The matching étagères and architectural lamps found in a catalog quietly play along.

Parsons-style side tables with open shelves multitask as a surface for a lamp and a place to display accessories (or board games!). These are from House Eclectic.

"I originally bought these black lacquered side tables in an attempt to **glamorize my bedroom.** They worked well there, but when Lauren talked me into buying these **quirky gilded brass lamps** at the Pier Antiques Show last year, I decided the side tables needed to move to the living room as they'd be **the perfect match** for the lamps." —*Suzanne*

Suzanne's splayed-arm sofa was most recently given new life, re-covered in a lush Rogers & Goffigon angora velvet. Pillows made from hand-dyed textiles are from Dransfield & Ross.

Just because you own a great pair of side tables and a beautiful pair of lamps doesn't mean they necessarily go together. More than anything else, the right lamp for a side table is all about proportion. A dinky little lamp is going to look off on a sturdy, commanding table, while a generous lamp will overwhelm a dainty table. In the living room, the end tables that flank your sofa should be close to the same height as the arm of the sofa.

# CREATE YOUR OWN MINI ART GALLERY

Covering your walls with art of different sizes, shapes, and provenances lets *you* be the curator. While it might look intimidating, probably the hardest part about creating a wall of art is collecting it. We found most of the art hanging above our sofa at flea markets for under one hundred dollars. To make your own art wall, start by laying out all the pieces you'd like to include (some of our favorite homemade galleries have mixed art, mirrors, hats, plates, and all sorts of other hanging objects). Next, measure the width and height of the space on the wall that you'd like to fill. Once you have the dimensions, use painter's tape to mark an identical one on the floor. Start placing your art one at a time until you find a configuration that you like. Then, one by one, hang each piece according to your plan. These gallery walls are not about perfection, so measuring the distance between each piece or frame is not necessary—just make sure you have a partner to help you eyeball it!

**OPPOSITE** The round mirror on the wall was found at a flea market. The metal star was made for Kedigian by a roofer on one of his design projects. **LEFT** On his windowsill, Kedigian placed objects from Mecox Gardens with an architectural ornament found at a construction site.

Finding pieces worthy of being reclaimed is often instinctive, but there is always a particular detail that stops you dead in your tracks. The color of wood and the skirt underneath this tabletop caught designer Garrow Kedigian's eye when he spotted this piece on the street in Boston years ago. Once ensconced in his apartment, this primitive table took on the role of a bedside table. Kedigian is a master accessorizer who expertly groups collectibles in interesting and utterly unforced ways. Here, personal framed photographs and a small alarm clock coexist among found objects. "Accessorizing is a real art," says Kedigian. "It takes a few tries to get it right, and I'm always revisiting it. A tabletop should never be fixed, but should be in flux over time, changing with the personality of seasons and your moods."

For a busy couple and their two young children, Kedigian completely updated this prewar apartment in New York City that had once been painted a Pepto-Bismol pink throughout. In the family room, he chose two different side tables to flank the sofa. On the right is a Regency-style round pedestal table, and on the left is a two-tiered square piece. "In this room, the window warranted the centerline of the sofa alignment, which left unequal spacing on either side for the tables," says Garrow Kedigian. "I took this as a cue to have a large end table with a lamp at one side to fill that corner and a floor lamp with a much smaller end table at the other side. Height is always a challenge when I do dissimilar end tables, but I do try to maintain the same height on both sides so the eye isn't weighted by one side or another." The lamps are also nonmatching with a blue and white Chinese tabletop lamp on the right, and on the left an innocuous standing lamp. Both have paper shades, which adds to their ease with each other in the same setting.

Kedigian masterfully mixes different patterns, textures, and hues, creating a room that is both cozy and sophisticated. In this room, the walls are painted Benjamin Moore's Pale Almond in keeping with Kedigian's technique of painting rooms in a neutral color palette to balance the dramatic artwork throughout the apartment.

"When accessorizing, I always ask the client to put out all their knickknacks on one side of the dining table, then I bring in some of my own and place them on the other side," explains Garrow Kedigian. "After all of the furniture is in place, I pluck from the dining table, item by item, placing things carefully but whimsically across the rooms." A room without accessories is like an outfit without shoes—and you can't go anywhere without your shoes on! There is a definite art to making the tabletops in your home sing, and there are a few golden rules that we like to follow. First, you want to use a variety of differently shaped objects of varying heights. Try to assemble them in odd numbers—symmetry is not always your friend! Taller pieces should go in the back and shorter ones in the front. Include a cool lamp on your tabletop. Not only will it provide a source of light, but it will also add height to the room. "Books are often the first element of accessorizing that add a primary layer of 'finishing-touch' personality to the room," says Kedigian.

## ACCESSORIZING A TABLE TOP

1. Keep accessories edited. Too many elements can look cluttered.

2. Add fresh flowers! We like to use unexpected varieties cut short and displayed in small vessels.

3. Choose accessories with varying heights, shapes, and textures.

4. Arrange lower pieces in front of higher ones to maximize visibility.

5. Candles are a great way to add style to any table on a budget.

"Even collectors of fine antiques will tell you that **great pieces** don't have to have historical provenance. 'Ordinary' pieces can make a **big impact** if they have an **element of surprise** about them." *—Suzanne*

A side table can also be placed against a wall in a large room—and if it has interesting details like the one interior designer Robert Couturier found in an antique store in western Connecticut, it absolutely should. We just love the red painted top of this whimsical table that is placed in a mix of other more authentic antiques. Sometimes choosing a piece is simply about knowing it will work in a room; it doesn't have to be an antique. "This table is nice, but really it's junk, and it works here by value of its colors: red, and black, and gold, which are the colors of the room," says Couturier. The weaving together of old and new, serious and not so serious, is what defines a stylish interior.

Couturier's collection of furniture and art is so refined, we were surprised to learn that this ornate black side table with gold detailing doesn't have much intrinsic value. It was found on a Saturday afternoon at one of his favorite antique haunts in Connecticut.

This master bedroom, designed by Garrow Kedigian, is a calm resting place for a very busy working couple. This classic two-tiered side table is the perfect height (mirroring the mattress height) for reaching over to grab a glass of water. Designed by Kedigian with a faux parchment finish reminiscent of mid-century-modern designer Jean-Michel Frank, the tables feature slightly radial corners for softness, and tiered gallery-style shelving to hold the owners' many bedside reading materials. For added flexibility, the tables are on casters, which makes them easy to move around the room.

The horizontal "biscuit" tufted headboard was custom designed by Kedigian and upholstered in a Nancy Corzine faux-bois textile. Its height is exaggerated to accommodate reading in bed. The animal-print bedcovering is Linx by Old World Weavers.

"In an otherwise monochromatic room, a shock of color is absolutely essential. Consider inserting color in the form of artwork, light fixtures, or even something as simple as a cashmere throw." — LAUREN

The turquoise blue Murano glass chandelier was found in a Paris flea market. A last-minute decision to add a modern, floral-patterned color reform carpet from ABC Carpet & Home added a much needed spark of youthfulness to this otherwise serious library/guest bedroom.

This chic study that, with its convertible sofa, doubles as a guest bedroom has a pair of lacquered side tables placed side by side in front of the sofa. Two matching side tables are a great alternative to your traditional coffee table, especially when you're working with a space that needs to serve more than one function. We selected these large square wood tables from one of our favorite furniture boutiques and had them custom-colored with a high-gloss chocolate-brown paint. When there isn't space for side tables on either side of the sofa, mounted lighting like this takes the place of table lamps.

Today's modern bathrooms are most often decorated with stone and tile work, but it's especially nice, if space allows, to include one wood furniture piece in the room. It immediately softens the feeling of the bathroom, making it all the more inviting for family and guests. The same table that works in your living room and your bedroom can also fit right into your bathroom. This faux-bamboo, wood chinoiserie table provides a convenient surface on which to place all the daily bath and beauty essentials, with a bottom shelf for stacking clean towels.

Luxurious towels from Matouk stacked below are an indulgence worth taking as they are truly the basis of an enjoyable bathroom experience.

# SIDE TABLE
# GLOSSARY

We find side tables that have at least one shelf and that are open in the back (to let light in and keep bulkiness at bay) to be the easiest to work with. A shelf to store books and magazines or to display some of your collectibles is both practical and chic. Round side tables are great for bringing another shape into living rooms and bedrooms that can easily get overrun with too many rectangular- and square-shaped pieces. If you're looking for the ultimate in flexibility, don't choose side tables that are too heavy looking or boxy. These pieces will only ever look like a night table. The key is to find pieces that are relatively simple in design, with either a drawer or a shelf, but probably not both.

**A**

**B**

**C**

**A** 1stdibs  **B** Suzanne Kasler for Hickory Chair  **C** Oly
**D** Design Within Reach  **E** Lee Jofa  **F** Oomph  **G** Williams Sonoma
**H** Alexa Hampton for Hickory Chair  **I** Crate & Barrel

# 7

# THE OCCASIONAL CHAIR

## WHERE TO USE IT

ENTRANCE FOYER, LIVING ROOM, DINING ROOM,
HOME OFFICE, BEDROOM

*T*he occasional chair is the one you pull out from a corner in your living room or out from against the wall to provide an extra seat for a guest. It's light and easily moved from one location to another. Occasional chairs are often used to bring in an element of wood, an unexpected shape, or, if upholstered, a new color or bold pattern into the space. While they're not considered must-haves in the most basic of floor plans, they're fantastic accessory-like pieces. The right occasional chair can move from the living room, where it serves as an interesting contrast to your basic club chairs and sofa, to the foyer, where two of them might frame a console table or a demilune, to the library, where it can be your desk chair. In fact, your dining-room-table chairs can often serve the role of the occasional chair. We have many chairs floating around the house that we once used at the dining-room table.

Every chair-back style from every period in history has a name, and familiarizing yourself with some of the most common ones is essential to becoming an educated consumer. In fact, learning the "language" of chairs is one of the most interesting parts of decorating. You'd be surprised by how much each detail reveals about the time during which the chairs were made. A certain kind of wood—mahogany, for

From English wingback and French Louis XVI chairs to American lattice-back and Greek klismos, the occasional chair provides a way to bring an authentic (or reproduction) period piece into your space that will immediately give your room an air of sophistication.

example—may have been more readily available during one period, while a certain crest or unique carving was popular during another. When choosing side chairs to place on either side of the fireplace or against a wall or around a table, it's okay to mix different furniture styles; just be sure that everything in the room has a common thread. In our own personal spaces, we prefer occasional chairs with open-worked backs that let light through but also add a graphic element to the room. If a space is in need of more color or pattern, we recommend choosing a chair that you can upholster either the seat cushion or the back of (or both). Slipcovers can be made for seat cushions and for chair backs, too, and they have the added advantage of washability.

The star of this magnificent 1916 Georgian-style house is its entrance hall. The walls are papered in Zuber's high-spirited L'Hindoustan pattern woodblock-printed wallpaper. Papers like these were originally created so that owners could feel as if they had traveled to faraway lands since, at the time, traveling long distances was difficult. We purchased a pair of 1940s klismos upholstered side chairs and had them re-covered in an updated Suzani textile to flank the doorway to the adjacent room.

Occasional chairs are sculptural additions. They soften a wide-open space like this one and can add an interesting architectural element to smaller-scale foyers. These are vintage from the 1940s.

Fashion designer Meredith German and her friend, interior decorator Barrie Benson, collaborated on Meredith's fabulously colorful New York City apartment. Meredith, originally from West Virginia, grew up a mile from the historic Dorothy Draper–decorated Greenbrier hotel. Meredith's proximity to a major interior-design landmark (growing up in a Carelton Varney–decorated house didn't hurt either) influenced much of the design of her own space—bright colors and bold florals abound. In fact, Meredith even has a little piece of the Greenbrier in her New York City apartment; she picked up her royal blue and white crewel sofa—formerly of the indoor pool area of the hotel—at a Dorothy Draper auction a few years ago (see page 13).

Inspired by the Greenbrier's bowling alley, Meredith and Barrie painted the wall near the entrance to the apartment with bold black-and-white stripes. The hothouse floral-upholstered Robsjohn-Gibbings chairs that sit in front of the striped wall are a nod to Dorothy Draper's singular and unmistakable style. "You must be careful not to place florals in the typical places," explains Barrie. "Florals on draperies can look a bit dated, but on small dining-room chairs, the pattern turns almost abstract." These occasional chairs create a lovely vignette as you walk into the apartment, but they can easily be moved into the dining room, where they are paired with a 1970s Pierre Cardin burled dining table, or into the living area as extra seating when guests are over.

The Robsjohn-Gibbings chairs are upholstered in a Carleton V floral and piped with a black patent leather to give the feminine fabric a punky kick. Benson artfully mixes the masculine and feminine, hanging a pair of ornate hydrangea sconces on strong black-and-white stripe-paneled walls.

**CLOCKWISE FROM TOP LEFT** Garrow Kedigian's pale blue vestibule, de Gournay wallpaper custom colored by Miles Redd, Barrie Benson mixes primary colors with aplomb, Robert Couturier combines peacock blue with hints of red.

# COLOR THEORY

In all of our favorite rooms, color plays a key role in creating a sense of harmony. Whether it's the color for the walls or the accessories in the room, we recommend using the color wheel as your guide. All color decisions stem from six primary colors: red, green, blue, purple, orange, and yellow. Perfect color synergy is reached either by incorporating two primary colors on opposite sides of the color wheel, like red and green, for example, or by choosing colors that are next to each other; pairing blue and light blue, or blue and blue-green, will always look right.

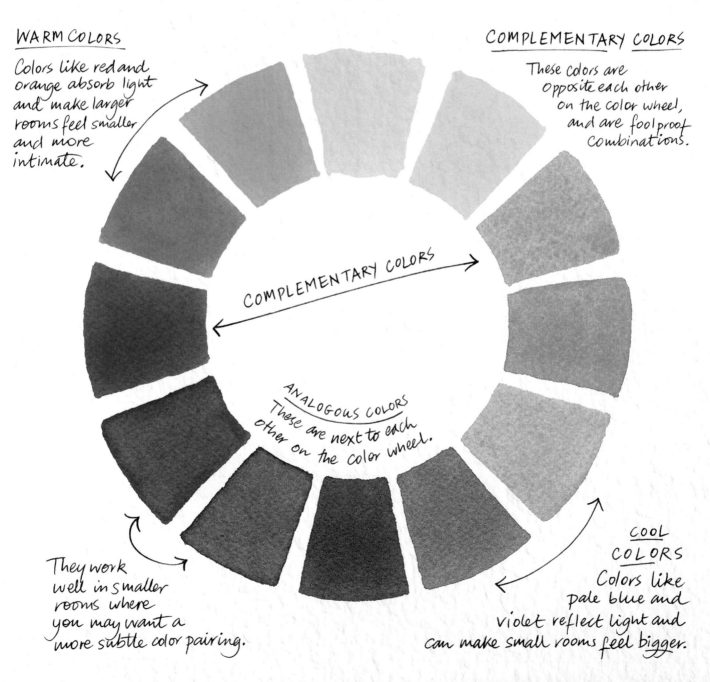

**WARM COLORS**

Colors like red and orange absorb light and make larger rooms feel smaller and more intimate.

**COMPLEMENTARY COLORS**

These colors are opposite each other on the color wheel, and are foolproof combinations.

COMPLEMENTARY COLORS

ANALOGOUS COLORS
These are next to each other on the color wheel.

They work well in smaller rooms where you may want a more subtle color pairing.

**COOL COLORS**

Colors like pale blue and violet reflect light and can make small rooms feel bigger.

Couturier had a custom stand made for this Louis XIV mirror. Couturier's goal was to "close the long perspective and at the same time abstractly continue it." It now looks as if the mirror is suspended in air when you enter the large room.

In the living room of Couturier's Manhattan apartment, the oak-and-porcelain table is by Jacques Adnet and Maurice Savin and the mirror is Louis XIV. A bold red and blue Turkish kilim is layered over a white rug.

In the living room of designer Robert Couturier's home, two French eighteenth-century armchairs signed by Jean-Baptiste Gourdin are the focal point of the room. Upholstered in a brown silk fabric, they are the epitome of chic. Couturier purchased these chairs in Paris, and they've lived many different lives in various rooms with corresponding upholstery. The cabriole legs curve outward and then inward in an inverted S shape. Couturier intentionally placed them turning away from each other so that they would each face their half of the living room. According to Couturier, "They look a bit like two twins having a fight! One has to keep a certain sense of surprise and humor."

# A GUIDE TO CHAIR-BACK STYLES

Become an educated antique buyer, not to mention a savvy flea-market scavenger, by being able to identify some of the most popular chair styles. Knowing the varying styles, and their importance, helps you spot a great look-alike— or better yet, the real thing. Here's a quick primer to help you name that style.

### Spool

These Gothic Revival chairs have limbs that look like rounded spools stacked one on top of another. Modern reproductions of this sculptural form have become popular in recent years.

### Windsor

Also known as the sack-back or hoop-back. Because they were often made of a combination of cheaper woods, you may find them painted dark green, brown or black, and sometimes even white.

### Louis XVI

An upholstered seat and chair back as well as tapered legs are the hallmarks of these chairs. Not to be confused with Louis XV chairs, with their cabriole legs that are curved in an inverted S shape.

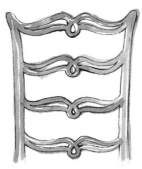

### Chippendale Ribbon (Ladder Back)

An American classic, the slats (horizontal pieces across the back) of this chair are curved and the centers are carved with unique designs. Its saddle seat is curved like a horse saddle for comfort.

## Hepplewhite Shield Back

The deeper and more intricate the carvings, the more valuable the chair is. If you're lucky enough to find the designer's name etched into the back of the seat rail, you've found an original piece of art.

## American Directoire (Sheraton)

Duncan Phyfe created some of the finest of this type of chair in the early 1800s. You can see exquisite examples of this style in the American Wing at the Metropolitan Museum of Art in New York City.

## French Empire

Decorative carvings or painted images of crowns, laurel leaves, torches, and mythological creatures are characteristic of this style, which originated in France in the early 1800s.

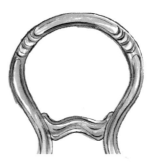

## Balloon Back

This Victorian-era chair merges the shield back and the circular back with a narrow, nipped waist. The roundness of the balloon back is the perfect contrast to a rectangular table.

These black French Empire–style chairs with painted Greek-key decoration immediately dress up the room. Ideally, a room should always have a mixture of wood and upholstered furniture. Too many upholstered pieces will make a room look heavy and unbalanced. Pairs of anything will create symmetry, but try not to carry the theme too far or else the room will start to look like you adhered to a formula.

The Greek-key French Empire–style chairs are from the Stamford Antique & Artisan Center. The glass coffee table is from Pottery Barn.

When not in use, one or two of these Louis XVI–inspired chairs live next to the fireplace. They serve as excellent extra seating options for guests as well as lovely complements to the pair of Swedish demilune tables. Positioning armchairs like these on either side of a fireplace can bring a nice feeling of symmetry to a room. Updating the upholstered seat and back with a contemporary stripe from Rogers & Goffigon makes them even more inviting.

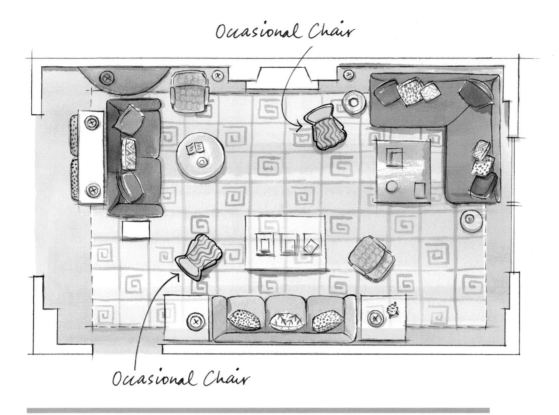

Occasional Chair

Occasional Chair

ABOVE Kedigian broke up this long living room into three separate seating areas.
OPPOSITE The custom Greek-key-motif rug from Stark echoes the geometric lines of the windowpanes behind.

In one of three seating arrangements in this living room, Garrow Kedigian created a custom banquette to fit seamlessly into the corner of the room. The eighteenth-century French caned seat and back armchair acts as a bridge between two seating areas—its mate sits on the opposite side of the room. A person sitting in this chair could be a part of multiple conversations in the room. It's important to any seating plan that no piece be too far away from the others. Remember: Everyone wants to be part of the party.

For this room, the launching pad for Kedigian was the chevron fabric on the kidney pillow on the sectional sofa. "The fabric of this pillow is an exploded, almost modern-scale chevron done in a cut velvet from F. Schumacher & Co.—it's one of my favorite fabrics of all time, and when the client reacted so well to it, I decided to orchestrate the entire room around that, sprinkling elements of its flavor throughout the room and in every corner!" says the designer.

Robert Couturier has an uncanny ability to assemble pieces—especially from his native France. In his living room, Couturier flawlessly groups one leather eighteenth-century Louis XVI armchair (far left) and an unusual 1930s white club chair with another eighteenth-century armchair upholstered in a brown silk (near right). The custom sofa, designed by Couturier, gives the space a thoroughly modern edge. While the blue and red velvet pillows on the sofa coordinate perfectly with the Turkish kilim, "This was not intentional at all," insists Couturier, "But good accidents happen!"

The artwork above the sofa is by Ron Agam, son of Israeli artist Yaacov Agam. Couturier commissioned two enormous, eight-by-eight-foot pieces for either side of this room.

The ceramic lamp on the desk is from Beeline Home. A collection of nine eighteenth-century English butterfly prints by Shaw & Nodder from Donogan Antiques Ltd. hangs above the vintage Baker desk. The tribal kilim is from Lillian August.

In the home office of the Georgian house, we paired a contemporary Louis Ghost chair with a 1950s walnut desk by Baker. The transparent occasional chair immediately makes this space feel less serious, providing a modern contrast to the traditional desk. The walls are painted a glossy red lacquer. Lacquered walls are a great way to dress up a room, but avoid trying this on modern sheetrock or unsmooth plaster walls as any imperfections will be magnified by high-shine paint.

"Once you've developed a **working knowledge** of chair-back styles, you're ready to **hunt like a pro.** There are few thrills greater than finding **a 'sleeper,'** that is, a valuable piece that no one except you recognizes." — *LAUREN*

Wₑ found these carved Chippendale chinoiserie upholstered side chairs on the lawn of Brimfield on a hot summer day. They had been painted a jarring bright green by their previous owner; we knew a coat of paint and some new upholstered cushions would freshen them up. They found a home in this breakfast room, where their carved backs speak to the off-white lattice-decorated walls.

The seat cushions are upholstered in Rose Cummings by Dessin Fournir "Banana Leaves."

# OCCASIONAL CHAIR
## GLOSSARY

The number of occasional chairs we have floating around our house and lined up in the basement borders on the absurd. But we're always finding ways of rationalizing bringing another one into our lives. Our favorite chairs available at retail are modern twists on traditional forms. The woven leather back of this klismos-inspired chair (F) and the quatrefoil motif of this neoclassical-style chair (D) are what make these pieces great. If you're looking for vintage occasional chairs, you can find both individual chairs and sets of chairs at flea markets and consignment stores all over the country—just don't expect them to date back to the early eighteenth century!

A

B

C

D

E

F

G

H

I

A Kindel  B Alexa Hampton for Hickory Chair  C Jonathan Adler
D Suzanne Kasler for Hickory Chair  E Victoria Hagan Home
F Beeline Home  G Mariette Himes Gomez for Hickory Chair
H Room & Board  I Zentique

# RESOURCES

## Furniture

### ABC Carpet & Home
881 Broadway
New York, NY 10003
212-473-3000
www.abchome.com

### Andrew Martin
222 East 59th Street
New York, NY 10022
212-688-4498

### Just Scandinavian
161 Hudson Street,
New York, NY 10013
212-334-2556

### Lillian August
32 Knight Street
Norwalk, CT 06851
203-847-3314
www.lillianaugust.com

### New York Design Center
200 Lexington Avenue
New York, NY 10016
212-679-9500
www.nydc.com

### Profiles
The New York Design Center
200 Lexington Avenue
Suite 1211
New York, NY 10016
212-699-6903

### Oly Studio
408 Greenwich Street
New York, NY 10013
www.olystudio.com

### Zentique, Inc.
6464 Warren Drive
Norcross, GA 30093
www.zentique.com

### Aesthetic Décor
www.aestheticdecor.com

**ANTHROPOLOGIE**
www.anthropolgie.com

**BAKER FURNITURE**
www.kohlerinteriors.com

**BALLARD DESIGNS**
www.ballarddesigns.com

**BLUE DOT MODERN FURNITURE**
www.bluedot.com

**BOLIER & COMPANY**
www.bolierco.com

**CISCO BROTHERS SUSTAINABLE FURNITURE**
www.ciscobrothers.com

**THE CONRAN SHOP**
www.conranusa.com

**CRATE & BARREL**
www.crateandbarrel.com

**DESIGN WITHIN REACH**
www.dwr.com

**FOUR HANDS**
www.fourhands.com

**GRAYPANTS**
www.graypants.com

**HICKORY CHAIR**
www.hickorychair.com

**HORCHOW**
www.horchow.com

**HOUSE ECLECTIC**
www.houseeclectic.com

**JONATHAN ADLER**
www.jonathanadler.com

**JULIAN CHICHESTER**
www.julianchichester.com

**KINDEL FURNITURE**
www.kindelfurniture.com

**LEE INDUSTRIES**
www.leeindustries.com

**McGuire Furniture**

www.kohlerinteriors.com

**One Kings Lane**

www.onekingslane.com

**Oomph**

www.oomphonline.com

**Paris Apartment**

www.theparisapartment.com

**Pier One Imports**

www.pier1.com

**Plexicraft**

www.plexicraft.com

**Restoration Hardware**

www.restorationhardware.com

**Room & Board**

www.roomandboard.com

**Robin Bruce**

www.robinbruce.com

**Roost**

www.roost.com

**Safavieh Home Furnishings**

www.safaviehhome.com

**Selamat Designs**

www.selamatdesigns.com

**Vaughan**

www.vaughandesigns.com

**Victoria Hagan Home Collection**

www.victoriahaganhome. com

**West Elm**

www.westelm.com

**Williams-Sonoma Home**

www.williams-sonoma.com

**Wisteria**

www.wisteria.com

**World's Away**

www.worlds_away.com

# Textiles and Wallpaper

## COLE & SON

Lee Jofa Inc.
201 Central Avenue South
Bethpage, NY 11714
800-453-3563
www.cole-and-son.com

## THE D & D BUILDING

979 Third Avenue
New York, NY 10022
212-838-7878

## DESSIN FOURNIR COLLECTIONS—
## ROSE CUMMINGS
## FINE ARTS BUILDING

232 East 59th Street
2nd Floor
New York, NY 10022
212-758-0844
www.dessinfournir.com

## DURALEE FABRICS, LTD.

175 Fifth Avenue
Bay Shore, NY 11706
800-275-3872
www.duralee.com

## FABRICUT INC.

9393 East 46th Street
Tulsa, OK 74145
800-999-8200
www.fabricut.com

## LEE JOFA

201 Central Avenue South
Bethpage, NY 11714
800-533-5632
www.leejofa.com

## OSBORNE & LITTLE

90 Commerce Road
Stamford, CT 06902
203-359-1599
www.osborneandlittle.com

## BRUNSCHWIG & FILS
The D & D Building
979 Third Avenue
New York, NY 10022
212-838-7878
www.brunschwig.com

## F. SCHUMACHER & CO.
The D & D Building
979 Third Avenue, Suite 832
New York, NY 10022
212-415-3900
www.fscumacher.com

## GLANT TEXTILES
979 Third Avenue
New York, NY 10022
800-884-5268
www.glant.com

## HINSON & COMPANY
The D & D Building
979 Third Avenue
New York, NY 10022
212-838-7878
www.hinsonco.com

## KNOLL TEXTILES
The D & D Building
979 Third Avenue
New York, NY 10022
800-343-5665
www.knolltextiles.com

## QUADRILLE
www.quadrillefabrics.com

## PHILLIP JEFFRIES
www.philliipjeffries.com

## SANDERSON & CO
www.sanderson.com

# Trimmings

## SAMUEL AND SONS PASSEMENTERIE
983 Third Avenue
New York, NY 10022
212-704-8000

## ROGERS & GOFFIGON
www.rogersandgoffigon.com

# Rugs

**MARK INC. FINE CARPETS**
34 East Putnam Avenue
Greenwich, CT 06830
800-227-0927
www.markinccarpets.com

**STARK CARPET CORP.**
979 Third Avenue
New York, NY 10022
212-752-9000
www.starkcarpet.com

**DASH & ALBERT**
www.dashandalbert.com

**MADELINE WEINRIB**
www.madelineweinrib.com

**THE RUG COMPANY**
www.therugcompany.com

# Lighting

**ARTERIORS HOME**
New York Design Center
200 Lexington Avenue, Suite 510
New York, NY 10016
www.arteriors home.com

**BEELINE HOME**
306 East 61th Street, 5th Floor
New York, NY 10065
212-935-5930
www.bunnywilliams.com/beeline

**REMAINS LIGHTING**
44 West Putnam Avenue
Greenwich, CT 06830
203-629-1000
www.remains.com

**THE URBAN ELECTRIC COMPANY**
2130 N. Hobson Avenue
North Charleston, SC 29405
www.urbanelectricco.com

**CHRISTOPHER SPITZMILLER**
www.christopherspitzmiller.com

## CIRCA LIGHTING

www.circalighting.com

## MOTTEGA LIGHTING

www.mottega.com

## NIERMANN WEEKS

www.niermannweeks.com

## VISUAL COMFORT

www.visualcomfort.com

# Tabletop, Home Accessories

## BUNGALOW

4 Sconset Square
Westport, CT 06880
203-227-4406

## DOVECOAT HOME

56 Post Road East
Westport, CT 06880
203-222-7500
www.dovecote-westport.com

## MECOX GARDENS

962 Lexington Avenue
New York, NY 10021
212-249-5301
www.mecoxgardens.com

## THE SILVER PEACOCK

1110 Park Avenue
New York, NY 10128
212-426-2610

## APARTMENT 48

www.apartment48.com

## BLUEFLY

www.bluefly.com

## CALVIN KLEIN HOME

www.calvinkleinhome.com

## FISHS EDDY

www.fishseddy.com

**GLOBAL TABLE**
www.globaltable.com

**GLOBAL VIEWS**
www.globalviews.com

**HB HOME**
www.hbhomedesign.com

**JOHN DERIAN**
www.johnderian.com

**KATE SPADE**
www.katespade.com

**NATURAL CURIOSITIES**
www.naturalcuriosities.com

# Linens

**FIG LINENS**
66 Post Road East
Westport, CT 06880
203-227-8669
www.figlinens.com

**JOHN ROBSHAW TEXTILES**
www.johnrobshaw.com

**KERRY CASSILL**
www.kerrycassill.com

**SERENA AND LILY**
www.serena&lily.com

# Decorative Pillows

**ABC CARPET & HOME**
888 Broadway 6th Floor
New York, NY 10003
212-473-3000

**ANKASA**
135 East 65th Street
New York, NY 10021
www.ankasa.com

**DRANSFIELD & ROSS**
54 West 21st Street
New York, NY 10010
212-741-7278
www.dransfieldandross.com

## MADELINE WEINRIB ATELIER

www.madelineweinrib.com

## MICHELLE VARIAN

27 Howard Street
New York, NY 10013
www.michelevarian.com

# Antiques and Vintage

## ANN MORRIS ANTIQUES

239 East 60th Street
New York, New York
212-755-3308

## BRASWELL GALLERIES

1 Muller Avenue
Norwalk, CT 06851
203-838-3319
www.braswellgalleries.com

## CABOT MILL ANTIQUES

14 Maine Street
Brunswick, ME 04011
207-725-2855
www.cabotiques.com

## CIRCA ANTIQUES

11 Riverside Avenue
Westport, CT 06880
www.circantiques.net

## THE STAMFORD ANTIQUES AND ARTISAN CENTER

69 Jefferson Street
Stamford, CT 06902
203-327-6022

## STRIPE VINTAGE MODERN

799 North East 125th Street
North Miami, FL 33161
305-893-8085
stripemiami@bellsouth.net

## 1STDIBS

www.1stdibs.com

**EBAY**
www.ebay.com

**GOODWILL**
www.shopgoodwill.com

**LONE RANGER ANTIQUES**
www.lonerangerantiques.com

**THE PIER ANTIQUES SHOW, PIER 94**
Americana and Antiques @ The Pier—
Stella Shows
www.stellashows.com

## Flea Markets

**BRIMFIELD ANTIQUE SHOW**
www.brimfieldshow.com

**MADISON-BOUCKVILLE ANTIQUES SHOW**
www.bouckvilleantiquesshows.com

**RHINEBECK ANTIQUES FAIR**
www.rhinebeckantiquesfair.com

## Paint

**BENJAMIN MOORE PAINTS**
www.benjaminmoore.com

**DONALD KAUFMAN COLOR**
www.donaldkaufmancolor.com

**FARROW & BALL**
www.farrowandball.com

**FINE PAINTS OF EUROPE**
www.finepaintsofeurope.com

## Custom Upholstery

**GERARDO GONZALEZ UPHOLSTERY**
350 Fairfield Avenue
Stamford, CT 06902
203-870-1400
www.gegouph.com

# Featured
# Designers

## BARRIE BENSON INTERIOR DESIGN

3821 Arborway
Charlotte, NC 28211
704-366-9916
www.barriebenson.com

## ROBERT COUTURIER & ASSOCIATES

69 Mercer Street #3
New York, NY 10012
212-463-7177
www. robertcouturier.com

## GARROW KEDIGIAN

64 East 80th Street
New York, NY 10075
212-517-8451
www.garrowkedigian.com

## LIEN LUU LTD.

304 West 92nd Street
New York, NY 10025
212-501-8617
lien@lienluultd.com

## SUZANNE McGRATH DESIGN, LLC.

14 Pine Lane
Rye, NY 10580
914-925-9088
www.goodbonesgreatpieces.com

## MILES REDD, LLC

77 Bleecker Street, Suite C111
New York, NY 10012
212-674-0902
info@milesredd.com

# Books

Joseph Aronson, *The New Encyclopedia of Furniture* (Crown Publishers, 1967)

Dorothy Draper, *Decorating Is Fun!* (Doubleday, Doran & Company, Inc., 1939 and First Pointed Leaf Press, LLC edition, 2006)

Judith Miller, *Miller's Antiques Encyclopedia* (Reed Consumer Books Limited, 1998)

Edith Wharton and Ogden Codman, Jr., *The Decoration of Houses* (W.W. Norton & Company, Inc., 1978)

Published in 2012 by Stewart, Tabori & Chang
An imprint of ABRAMS

Library of Congress Cataloging-in-Publication Data

McGrath, Suzanne.
Good bones, great pieces : the seven essential pieces that will carry you
through a lifetime / Suzanne and Lauren McGrath ; photographs by Lucas Allen.
   p. cm.
  ISBN 978-1-58479-957-3
1.  Furniture. 2.  Interior decoration.  I. McGrath, Lauren. II. Allen, Lucas. III.
Title. IV. Title: Seven essential pieces that will carry you through a lifetime.
  NK2115.5.F77M39 2012
  747—dc23

           2011045354

Editor: Dervla Kelly
Designer: Amy Sly
Production Manager: Tina Cameron

The text of this book was composed in Fournier, Gotham, and Kievit.

Printed and bound in China

10 9 8 7 6 5 4 3 2 1

Stewart, Tabori & Chang books are available at special discounts when purchased
in quantity for premiums and promotions as well as fundraising or educational
use. Special editions can also be created to specification. For details, contact
specialsales@abramsbooks.com or the address below.

# ABRAMS
THE ART OF BOOKS SINCE 1949
115 West 18th Street
New York, NY 10011
www.abramsbooks.com